ISBN 978-0-260-87852-6
PIBN 10979798

BRANCH OF RESEARCH

April, 1930

CONTENTS

ALLEGHENY FOREST EXPERIMENT STATION (March & April)

General

A schedule of insurance rates on plantations has been received from the company which was referred to in an earlier report as insuring forest land. The schedule is as follows:

BASIS RATE $2.00

ACREAGE
- (a) Basis rate is computed on tract of 150 acres.
- (b) For every twenty-five acres or fraction thereof less than 150 acres, deduct 5% of basis rate.
- (c) For every twenty-five acres or fraction thereof more than 150 acres, add 5% of basis rate.
- (d) Size of tracts may be reduced by barriers as hereinafter set forth.

BARRIERS
- (a) A barrier sufficient to reduce size of tract or to warrant other credit must be sixteen feet or more in width, twelve feet of which must be maintained at all times either devoid of vegetation by cultivation or cleared in the spring and fall, before and after the period of growth, in such manner as is expedient.

CREDITS
- (a) Tract within vision from fire tower......................... .10
- (b) Watchman living adjacent to insured tract.................... .10
- (c) Forest Fire Warden in vicinity or district.................. .15
- (d) Posting prominently every 100 years around tract and on all public and private roads and byways on or bordering said tract, placards warning against carelessness with fire and trespass....................................... .05
- (e) Barriers on all sides....................................... .50

CHARGES
- (a) Steam railroads having more than 1% grade through or adjacent to tract.. .75
- (b) Portable steam sawmill on insured tract or adjacent lands.... .75
- (c) If exposed by adjacent timber lands including slashings, cut-over tracts, etc., either owned by assured or others..... .25

(Over)

The Company offering the above rate schedule has insured a considerable acreage of plantations for the Clearfield Bituminous Coal Corporation of Indiana, Pa. The latter Corporation has recently issued, evidently for propaganda purposes, a booklet on their woodland and their forestry operations.

Mr. L. W. R. Jackson, who has been doing graduate work at the University of Pennsylvania in the past year, will be reinstated in the Bureau of Plant Industry on July 1, and has accepted one of the new Philadelphia assignments.

Hough visited the tract controlled by the Bureau of Animal Industry at Beltsville, Md., and finds that although there is a considerable area of woodland suitable for experimentation, and although the Bureau is quite cordial in its offers of this tract for experimental purposes, there is no positive assurance that the ground will not eventually be cleared for new pastures. Under the circumstances we should certainly be in no hurry to consider this tract as a branch station. Although almost entirely in the coastal plain, and on the western shore of the Chesapeake Bay, where we have tentatively thought we would like to locate a branch station, this tract does not appear to be thoroughly typical, because of the lack of Virginia pine.

Forestation

Wood and McComb planted about 3000 seedlings of 5 different species at Camp Ockanickon during the latter part of March. The species included about 500 each of white, red, jack, and pitch pines, and about 800 short-leaf pine. The coniferous seedlings were planted in openings of an 8-year old hardwood sprout stand, and were distributed at the rate of about 500 to the acre. The hardwood growth was clean cut from only about half an acre out of the 5½ acres planted, but was cut back in the immediate neighborhood of the planted seedlings on the rest of the area. Because of the irregular spacing it was absolutely essential to mark the location of each seedling with a conspicuous marker and painted white cedar poles were used for this purpose. Later the poles were tagged with aluminum tags, at the rate of about 750 a day, for two men. The jack pine, which had already started to lengthen its terminal buds, was very badly injured by what appear to have been rabbits; about 37% of the seedlings were killed outright and an additional 13% may die. Apparently the trees were planted at the time when very little green vegetation had yet developed, and on that account fell a victim before the other species, which had not as yet lengthened their winter buds.

literature on the subject of diameter distribution in even-aged and un-even-aged stands, have cleared up a number of points that have been puzzling us. The facts so far unearthed concerning white pine certainly encourage us to examine more second-growth and original stands (reconstructed from stumps) of this species.

Wood completed an office report on the white pine reproduction in a tract near Dushore, Pa.; here, as further west in our territory, the period during which white pine finds conditions satisfactory for germination of seed and survival of seedlings is comparatively short.

-----#-----

APPALACHIAN FOREST EXPERIMENT STATION

Bent Creek Forest

Activities on the experimental forest are increasing with the advance of the season. The forest biologist is busy there all the time. Considerable work on the fire damage and forestation projects have been going on, and regular records of the development and growth of vegetation on the forest are being kept.

A working plan for the management of the forest by Buell attempts to combine on the same area some of the features of a demonstration forest with the sample plots and experimental work which are its chief reasons for being. The plan states that "it is proposed to handle work on the forest so that (1) all experiments will be located in forest types and conditions appropriate to them, (2) adequate space will be provided in advance for each experiment without the possibility of interference between experiments, and (3) the experiments will serve to best advantage gradually to develop the whole forest in such a way that sequences can be followed and related experiments most easily compared."

In connection with the tests of species project, an experiment in converting abandoned old fields which are restocking to a scattered growth of limby pitch, shortleaf, and Virginia pine was begun this spring. Two plantations of about an acre each were made in a ridge pasture. Fifteen hundred red pine (3-0) transplants were used in one plantation, and 1200 southern balsam fir (3-0) in the other. The trees were spaced evenly over the areas without regard to the volunteer stand present. After the planting the overstory was removed over a part of the area by felling the trees; on another part the small trees were cut, and the larger ones girdled; on a third part the overstory was allowed to remain. Slash was lopped but allowed to remain on the plots.

A tally of the volunteer stand showed 488 trees per acre 4.5 feet tall and taller. Only 58 of these were over 6 inches d.b.h. Taper measurements were made on a number of the felled pines. Naturally they have very rapid taper, and were very limby. The trees averaged 15 years old; very few of them were over 25 feet high.

Phenology

The oaks and pines at the elevation of Bent Creek are at least two weeks in seasonal development behind those 150 feet in elevation above the creek. By the last of April the scarlet oaks on the middle and upper slopes on the forest were half out in full leaf, the white oak leaf blades were fully spread out, yellow poplar was three-fourths in full leaf, the Virginia pine was through shedding pollen, and the pollen shedding of the pitch pine was at its height. At the creek level, the scarlet oak buds had just begun to burst, the white oaks were still dormant, the yellow poplar had started growth, but had been frosted back, the Virginia pine had started to shed pollen, but the staminate cones of the other pines were still immature. On April 24 and 25 there were severe frosts along Bent Creek, the temperature dropping as low as 26° F. according to the thermograph records. At the creek level the young leaves of yellow poplar, sassafras, and benzoin were frozen. Red maple and dogwood were uninjured; the oak buds were not far enough advanced to be harmed. At elevations greater than 100 or 150 feet above the creek there was no frost damage.

Fire Damage to Soils

April was a dangerous fire period in the region near Asheville and advantage was taken of it to complete the controlled spring burning experiment at Bent Creek.

The controlled burning experiment being conducted at Bent Creek consists of four plots, a check plot, a spring burning, a fall burning, and a raking plot. The raking plot has been included to investigate the effects of the removal of litter unaccompanied by fire.

The spring burning area was burned over on April 10. The weather during the preceding two weeks had been very dry and conditions were good for a representative burn. Early afternoon was chosen as the best time for burning and so the fire was touched off at 1:45 p.m. It burned briskly and sometimes advanced rather rapidly. By 2:30 the entire area, about 2 acres, had burned over. An anemometer set up at the plot recorded $1\frac{1}{2}$ miles of wind per hour while the fire was burning, an increase of only half a mile per hour over the velocity recorded for the half hour preceding. This is hardly a significant indication of the effect of the fire

on wind movement. The effect of the fire on air currents in small pockets
surrounded by fire was, however, rather spectacular, the flames rising in
a whirling current of air to heights of 25 to 30 feet.

The fire advanced before the wind up the 25% slope at the rate of
about 12 feet per minute. According to local residents familiar with fire
behavior in the region, this is not fast and yet the burn was rather in-
tense. They allowed that on long steep slopes where the fire would affect
wind movement the rate might be three to four times as great.

The intensity of flame temperatures and of the fire generally are
evidenced by the melting of aluminum tags placed at $4\frac{1}{2}$ feet above the
ground. Two weeks after the fire the crowns of pines on the plot were
scared and brown to heights of 50 feet. Whether this was due directly to
high temperatures or to the desiccating action of the large volumes of hot
air above the fire was not determined.

In preparing the fire lines surrounding the plot preparatory to
burning, some interesting observations were made. Three methods were used.
Along one side the litter had been raked last fall to the center of a strip
a quarter chain wide but left unburned until this spring. The resulting
heap of leaves retained moisture in the lower levels so that a good burn
was not obtained even though the leaves were turned over twice in the two
days preceding the burning. Another method of constructing the fire-lines
was identical with the first except that the leaves were burned the same
day they were raked. The third method was to rake the litter away from
the center of the quarter-chain-wide strip leaving about 5 feet undisturbed , which was later burned.

Observations on the time needed for construction and on the effectiveness of the lines led to the conclusion that the most economical and
efficient fire-lines for protection of plots can be made by raking the
litter from a strip 12 to 15 feet wide away from the direction of danger
and then cutting a line a few feet wide in the center of the raked strip
through the duff to the mineral soil.

Planting Work

On April 24 Sims with a crew of 6 men made a hurried trip to the
planting site on Mt. Mitchell and put in 10 one-chain-square test plots.
Five species were used: Norway pine, Japanese larch, white spruce, Douglas fir, and western red cedar.

At Bent Creek in addition to the plantations of balsam and red pine
which have already been mentioned, plantings of 12 different species were
added to the arboretum.

At the Canton nurseries selected stock from the 1927 and 1928 seed
beds was transplanted.

Forest Pathology

Nelson went to Mt. Mitchell with Sims on the 24th and supervised the planting of 350 Oriental chestnuts there. He received a shipment of 2000 trees of Asiatic species of Castanea to be planted in the vicinity of Asheville to test their immunity to the chestnut blight, their success in this climate, and their suitability as timber trees. The remainder of the trees were planted at Bent Creek.

Methods of Cutting--Hardwoods

Word has been received from Supervisor Sears, of the Natural Bridge National Forest, that fires which occurred April 11-14 destroyed all of the "sanitation cuttings" and sample plot work done in the McFalls Creek area in 1929. The fire has apparently wiped out the three series of plots-- one series consisting of three one-acre plots, the others of smaller paired plots--which were described in the report for July, 1929. It also destroyed an unusually fine reproduction, chiefly of white pine and yellow poplar, much of which had been given increased space and light by the "sanitation cutting."

Costal Plain Work

Korstian and MacKinney spent the first two days of April with the Cornell senior forestry students in their spring camp at Witherbee, South Carolina. During this time a search was made for areas cut over 30 to 50 years ago by the old Burton Lumber Company which might be suitable for the proposed selective logging study next fall. One area was found on the lands of the North State Lumber Company which offers possibilities and which will be examined in June by R. D. Garver of the Forest Products Laboratory.

With the help of Professor E. Fritz and Graduate Students Wilm and Olsen, Korstian and MacKinney also reexamined six loblolly pine growth sample plots at Witherbee. These plots were established in 1905 on the cuttings of the Burton Lumber Company and have been examined periodically since then. The data will be compiled and prepared for publication in the near future.

A single day, April 4, was spent at Lanes, South Carolina. The quadrats on the controlled burning plots were reexamined, and Hursh, who was with the coastal plain party, studied the soil on the burned and unburned areas.

During the second week of the month the suitability of the forested portions of the Clemson College Coastal Experiment Station at Drainland, South Carolina, for future forest research was examined. A rough

survey and a type and age class map were made for the portions of the
tract which are being devoted to forest experiments and timber production, and Hursh studied the soils in the area. The total available
area of 157 acres is in three contiguous tracts, and is occupied mainly
by longleaf pine reproduction and poles, and by loblolly pine reproduction and poles.

This tract offers good possibilities for intensive work because
of (1) State ownership insuring permanency, (2) present satisfactory forest conditions, (3) guaranteed fire protection, and (4) the excellent cooperative spirit displayed by Clemson College.

A day at Drainland was spent helping W. R. Mattoon obtain data on
seedspots which were established on the area in 1916-1917. Mattoon is
planning to prepare a report rounding up the results of these reseeding
experiments before the Appalachian Station takes up experimental work on
the tract.

In addition, two new one-third-acre permanent sample plots were established on the Clemson College lands for the controlled burning project.
One of these was on an area which has been burned annually for the last
14 years, and the other, on an adjacent area which has remained unburned
for 13 years. Records beginning in 1916 were available for a number of
trees on each of these plots.

During the third week of the month, MacKinney and Larsen reexamined
the selective logging sample plots at Windsor, North Carolina, which were
cut over last winter. The reproduction quadrats were examined to determine the amount of damage done to advance reproduction by logging.

------#------

CALIFORNIA FOREST EXPERIMENT STATION (March)

General

The most interesting feature of the month was the two-day conference on the consumptive use of water, which met in Los Angeles on the 27th
and 28th. The conference was under the auspices of the Committee on Con-
tributions to Ground Water Supplies from Rainfall and by Spreading of
Streams, of the Irrigation Division of the American Society of Civil Engineers. For this purpose the items considered as consumptive use constitu-
ted a pretty heterogeneous array, varying from those factors in water producing areas constituting the spread between the amount of water received
from rains and the amount deliverable from the area, to those accounting
for all phases of use or loss of the water delivered upon agricultural
water consuming areas. The essential thing from our point of view, however,

was that the way was opened for candid consideration of the factors constituting the "influences" of vegetative cover upon the disposition of
precipitation waters, and for getting into the engineer's picture the
price which must be paid, in any attempt to save the water consumed by
the chaparral, through burning or otherwise destroying the cover.

The first day's session was devoted to presentation of research
work, in the morning that of the horticulturists and irrigation engineers,
dealing with the water requirements of orchard trees and crop plants, the
afternoon that of the foresters as a joint presentation by the Experiment
Station and University of California, dealing with the wild plants of
water producing areas. The second day was devoted to the presentation by
practical workers, engineers, agriculturists, and foresters of their needs,
and their appraisal of how far the research described on the first day met
those needs.

The registered attendance at the meetings was 110. On Saturday
also there was held a field trip, in which about 20 persons participated,
to see the experimental work of the Forest Experiment Station at Devil
Canyon, the U. S. Division of Agricultural Engineering experiments in
water penetration, and the water spreading grounds on the Santa Ana River.
The party were also guests by invitation of Forest Supervisor Elliott at
the dinner and dedication of the Starke forest plantation at the Lytle
Creek Ranger Station of the San Bernardino National Forest.

Management

Preparation for a long field season has been the chief occupation
of Dunning and Hasel. One new working plan has been written and five old
ones rewritten. Tracing of the three large detailed maps of the 1929
Stanislaus Mc plots is being completed by Hasel. These must be checked
over in the field this spring to record slash disposal damage. About 1600
of the 1940 mil-acre quadrat maps have been inked in preparation for the
annual recharting. Eleven more Mc working plans remain to be rewritten
before reexaminations start.

Two sets of new quadrat mapping frames were made to include some
new notions acquired during past field work. A more convenient holder for
individual tree sheet forms (F-561) was also manufactured as well as some
alidade sights to fit on ordinary triangular engineers scales. These
knick-knacks assume considerable importance at 5-year intervals when many
plots must be examined in a brief period.

Bachman from the Sierra came to the Station on March 24 to compile
the data from two Mc plots established by the Forest personnel in 1929.
These plots represent Forest Service and light economic selection cutting
in the sugar pine - fir type. A careful study of felling and grading damage was made, which is of particular interest because electric donkeys
were used in yarding.

Mensuration

Reinecke has been making an analysis of the effect of composition on yield of even-aged, second-growth, mixed conifer stands in the Sierras. A multiple curvilinear correlation on 225 plots, collected by Dunning and others, shows that with high percentages of western yellow and sugar pines, the total basal area is 10 - 15 per cent above average, while high percentages of Douglas fir reduce the total basal area to 10 - 15 per cent below average. White fir and incense cedar maintain the average. The final correlation coefficient was .785.

Cover Type Map

During the month four 2-man crews have been in the field, two on the Santa Barbara National Forest and one each in Riverside and Monterey counties. In addition one district ranger has been working independently on the Cleveland National Forest.

The project personnel augmented during the winter months by cooperation from State, County, and Federal agencies was decreased by three men the last week of March. Two district rangers and one assistant provided by the Southern Forests could no longer be spared from their administrative duties. However, two Federal rangers assigned from Tahoe and Stanislaus Forests and two State rangers will continue on until May 1.

Since the first of the year approximately the following area has been covered.

Los Angeles County	500	sq. miles
Santa Barbara National Forest	430	" "
Cleveland " "	80	" "
Riverside County	100	
Monterey "	90	'
Total	1,100	" "

In completing this area two men from the Experiment Station have been working continuously. In addition, the following cooperation was had:

Los Angeles County: 2 men and 2 automobiles for 2 months.
State Division of Forestry: 2 men and 2 automobiles for 1 month.
U. S. Forest Service Administrative Organization: 5 men and 3 automobiles for 2 months.

Forest Influences

San Dimas Installation

During the first part of March Lowdermilk and Sundling installed a complete surficial run-off and erosion experimental set-up in San Dimas Canyon. This is a cooperative experiment, between the Los Angeles County Conservation Association, the Forest Supervisor of the Angeles National Forest, the San Dimas Water Company, Mr. A. L. Sonderregger, consulting hydraulic engineer, and the California Forest Experiment Station. The installation comprises two plots from which a heavy cover of chaparral was cut and burned and two plots within similar but undisturbed chaparral of excellent development in which there has been no fire for at least 40 years.

The San Dimas Water Company is to install a sprinkling device which will permit the application of artificial rain. This installation will answer questions relating to comparative surficial run-off, erosion,and interception. It will not answer the question of how much water chaparral vegetation is transpiring - which is now pressing for an answer. It is pla ned to install a battery of lysi-phytometers and rain retention pans also at this site so as to complete an experimental installation for the study of the influences of chaparral on the disposition of meteoric waters.

Sundling also spent a week at the North Fork installation, taking soil moisture samples and charting vegetation on the covered plots. The barren plots yielded in a storm of 1.7 inches of rain 3.9 and 7.1 cubic feet of run-off respectively, whereas the covered plots yielded 0.0 and 0.1 cubic feet respectively. It is interesting to note that the bare plot yielding the more run-off (7.1 cu. ft.) has a slightly less gradient than the other and likewise showed more gullying. This is due it appears to a heavier burn which resulted in removing a larger fraction of included organic material. New leads were obtained from this inspection which make i appear that it will be possible to single out factors influencing the init tion of erosive processes. There is enough possibility that this may thro new light on the whole problem to make it worth while to follow up.

Consumptive Use of Water by Chaparral Vegetation

At the Los Angeles conference Lowdermilk presented a paper of which the following passages are quoted from the portion devoted specifica ly to evaporation and transpiration losses.

Retention or Consumptive Use

The third factor in the disposition of meteoric waters is retentio of water by the catchment area. It is also designated "consumptive use". Retention or consumptive use may be further divided into:

            i.   Evaporation
           ii.   Transpiration
          iii.   Water of combination
           iv.   Abysmal seepage

Transpiration

Transpiration includes water taken up by roots and given off from
the aerial parts of plants. The principal portion of transpiration is
given off through leaves. The stems as well as dead plants give off small
quantites of moisture to the atmosphere.

As far as is known no studies of transpiration have been made which
serve to indicate the transpiration losses from chaparral forests by area
in southern California. Data including the combined amount of transpiration
and evaporation, do not permit the segregation into component values without
experimental study.

The following general features of the problem have received consideration in the present undertaking by the California Forest Experiment Station
to study transpiration losses experimentally. This analysis is presented
for discussion by this group. It is essential that all phases of the problem be considered in conducting experimental determinations.

The first feature to be considered is the relation of the rainy to
the growing season. Winter rains and dry summers simplify this problem in
one particular. The degree of arrested growth in winter varies with altitude and latitude. In the valleys of southern California the growth of ever-
green plants is much retarded or completely stopped. The transpiration losses during winter are much less than during the favorable growing temperatures of summer. At increasing altitudes up canyons and mountain slopes
transpiration decreases to a minimum at snow line. Likewise the length of
the growing season varies in length with altitude, being longest, of course,
at valley elevations.

Growing and rainy seasons are coincident to a varying extent. Over-
laps of favorable growing temperatures above a diurnal average of 40° F.
(Livingston and Shreve 1921), and rainy seasons vary also with altitude. It
is necessary to determine the importance of transpiration during the overlap
periods for the entire range in altitude.

The second important feature of the problem in southern California
is the recognition of two major types of vegetation included within the
watersheds of the region. They are, (1) the vegetation confined to drained
slopes, and (2) the canyon bottom or stream side vegetation which enjoys
sub-irrigation throughout most or the entire period of favorable growing
temperatures. The sharp division between these two types is discernable
from vantage points on ridges. Type maps now being made under the supervi-
sion of A. E. Wieslander of the California Forest Experiment Station clearl

-13-

show the type boundaries and the comparative area covered by each type. These distinctions become less conspicuous with increase in altitude above the cloud line.

These two types of vegetation are believed to have widely different quantities of water at their disposal. On the drained slopes the water holding capacity or field capacity of the soil less the moisture at the wilting point represents all the moisture available to vegetation after the last rain in spring. After the chaparral forest has extracted the easily available moisture it must survive on very small amounts of moisture throughout the remainder of long seasons favorable to growth. Pearson (1926) found that pine (Pinus ponderosa) and Rocky Mountain Douglas fir (Pseudotsuga taxifolia) rapidly consume available water, but are capable of surviving for long periods of time on very small quantities of moisture. It seems probable that chaparral vegetation is required to do this. Its dwarfed form is doubtless a response to the limiting factor of moisture.

On the contrary, the vegetation in canyon bottoms has all the water it can use at its disposal throughout the summer. The species of the vegetation are unmistakable indicators of this condition. They are willows, alders, sycamores, grapevines, all of which transpire great quantities of water which Rowe (1924) found at the mouth of White Water River to approximate the evaporation from a free water surface, a total of about 8 acre feet per year.

These considerations have an important bearing on explanations of observed increased flow in streams and the opening of small springs at the lower ends of willow flats following forest fires. It is, for this reason, probable that such increases in flow come from a reduction in transpiration losses from the subirrigated canyon bottom vegetation rather than from the chaparral vegetation on drained slopes. In fact, it is impossible to see how a fire would cause the slope soils to give up any of their capillary water to underground flow. On the contrary forest fires can be expected to increase evaporation from the soil. Conspicuous soil slides following fires are indicative of a powder dry condition of soil which fire has produc

More significant still is a consideration of the possibility of carry ing field capacity water in drained soils from one rainy season to another. To increase the yield of water from drained slopes it is necessary to hold over such increases in the soil to the succeeding rainy season, where it is effective in increasing the gravity flow. Summer fires are followed by the rainy season. Under light intensities of rain erosion may not be conspicuous, but under heavy intensities accelerated erosion is a common associated phenomenon with burned watersheds. During the following spring burns are r clothed with vegetation in varying degrees. We need to know more accurat i the density and kind of regrowth. The succession studies of C. J. Kraebel of the Station are indicating important information on this point. Some types of growth such as the chamise (Adenostoma fasciculatum) and oak

-14-

(Quercus dumosa)sprout vigorously following fires. It is common for a lux-
uriant growth of herbaceous vegetation to follow fires to be gradually suc-
ceeded within about 5 years with the woody chaparral species which formed
the original cover. The succession of seeded vegetation is slower on large
burns, due in all probability to lack of disseminated plant seed.

The regrowth on burns in the first season, as well as in succeeding
years, has before it a long season with temperatures favorable for growth.
Temperature is not a limiting factor. The regrowth can be expected, therefore, to grow as long as it has moisture available in the soil. In the
case of sprouting vegetation the reach of the roots doubtless is identical
with that of the plants before the fire. In the case of herbaceous vegetation and new woody plants from seed the roots may or may not reach the
depths of the former cover. Yet it seems probable that growth would continue until all available moisture within the root zone was consumed. Thus
the height of vegetation is not concluded to be an index of the amount of
transpiration on the drained slopes. In fact it appears probable that the
sprouting plants transpire more energetically and more water than the mature
plants. Experimental determinations are needed to check this hypothesis,
which is formulated on an analysis of the factors involved in the problem.

In order, therefore, to increase the yield of water from the drained
slopes, it would seem to be necessary to kill the vegetation permanently.
Instances exist in California where this has been done by smelter fumes.
The Kennett area north of Redding is a good example. It is more than probable that the yield in run-off has been increased in this area over the
pre-smelter days. This interesting area, incidentally, offers an unparal-
leled opportunity to test experimentally the effect of the total destruc-
tion of the mantle of vegetation on the yield of water from watersheds.
Certainly the evidence is not sufficient to advocate the employment of
smelter fumes to increase water supply with the attendant acceleration of
erosion, increased turbulency of stream discharge and other consequences
to agriculture.

It follows that a very fruitful source for increased yield of water
is the summer growing canyon bottom vegetation. To cut it or kill it by
fire would be both unsatisfactory and would at best net only temporary increases. The method which has been employed in a number of instances, of
robbing this vegetation of the drainage flow by collecting and piping it
out of the canyon offers the greatest promise. This method is suggested
as a means of increasing the yield of water from mountain watersheds.

Evaporation

Evaporation may be the most important factor in retention or consumptive use in southern California. When considered as direct losses
from wetted surfaces it comprises:

-15-

1. Interception by vegetation and its litter
2. Interception by soils

The ratio of evaporation to transpiration will depend on the characteristics of precipitation. If all rain in southern California should occur as 0.5 inch storms one week apart evaporation would account for practically the total supply of meteoric waters. The manner of occurrence of precipitation is doubtless of more importance in determining the supply of underground water than the presence or absence of vegetation on a watershed. Any determinations of the yield of streamflow from rainfall, which does not take into account this feature of the problem not only is incomplete but may actually mislead.

Accordingly determinations of the factors controlling the effectiveness of rainfall are of more importance than those of total amount. The studies of the interception of vegetation by Engler (1919), Munns (1921), Bates and Henry (1928), and Hirate (1929) all indicate that light rains scarcely reach the ground. Only the heavier falls replenish soil moisture.

Exposed bare soils function in a way similar to that of vegetation. The soil layer of the most active capillary movement including a depth to approximately 8 inches acts in a way analogous to the interception of vegetation. Rains which do not wet below this depth may be lost by evaporation if a few days of clear weather follow storms.

Thus a comparison of the evaporation losses by a mantle of vegetation and by bare soil involves a weighing of relative values. Engler (1919) found as had Ebermayer (1876) and Henri (1908) that whereas the mantle of vegetation reduces the contribution of water to the soil, yet it reduced the evaporation of such supplies that were absorbed by the soil in comparison with the evaporation losses from bare soils.

This phase of the problem requires careful experimentation. Experimental studies were undertaken by the California Forest Experiment Station in 1929 to answer some of the questions which have been raised here. The principal objective is to discover the portion of a season's precipitation by amounts and intensities of storms, which passes through vegetation, litter layers, and layers of soil of different depths up to 3 feet. Instruments are designed to measure the following factors:

1. Interception of rain by vegetation
2. Amounts of rain which pass through
   (a) litter layers
   (b) litter and soils of different depths
   (c) bare soil of different depths
3. Water losses from soil columns 3 feet deep by evaporation, and by transpiration.

A serious experimental difficulty is encountered in these installations. It is the impounding of water by film forces at the interface between water and air of a broken column of soil. Experimental manipulation is being tried to bridge this interface by a system of wicks which connect the soil with a water trap. The success of the device is yet uncertain.

In conjunction with this instrumentation soil moisture sampling is being conducted in a preliminary way at 3 sampling areas. A general systematic attack on the sampling of soil within and without vegetation throughout the year is planned for this and the following year.

Southern California
(February and March)

The prevalence of hot dry weather and winds during early February not only made planting and stock distribution from the nursery impossible but threatened to start growth in the waiting stock. To prevent the huge losses which would have been inevitable under continuance of these conditions it was decided to lift all stock at once and place it in cold storage to await suitable planting weather. Space was obtained in a San Bernardino ice plant for storage at 38° F. Transplants were lifted first and the seedlings were heavily shaded to retard the spring call of direct sunlight.

The exceptional size of this year's transplant stock has been mentioned in previous reports. Digging soon disclosed that the root systems were proportionately deep and vigorous, and the lifting operation proved slow and costly in consequence. A portable burlap-covered shelter eight feet square had to be built to house digging operations against wind and sun. The further precaution of puddling all roots was also resorted to, good clay for the purpose having been discovered within a hundred yards of the nursery. The trees were packed with shingle tow exactly as for shipment, in bundles of 250 and 300, making possible their withdrawal from storage in any quantity for experimental purposes or for distribution to the counties. Thus is being put into practice the results of the study conducted by the Pacific Northwest Station with Wind River nursery stock.

Products

Woods and Mill Study

Computing assistants are now well under way on the final lap of the relay race we have been running since last fall, to get our data on 8600 logs ready for the punch card operators. They are summarizing the green chain tally records by thickness and width groups in such manner

that the final tabulations will segregate for the higher grades, six
thicknesses from 4/4 to 16/4, and within each thickness, three width
groups, viz., 4 to 11 inches, 12 to 19 inches, and 20 inches to wider.
The common grades are divided only into 4/4 x A/W, 5/4 and thicker x
4 to 10" wide, and 5/4 and thicker x 12" and wider, unless finer sub-
divisions can be made without using extra cards on the basis of the
groups shown for any particular log in the upper grades. The card
design finally adopted lists all grades complete on one card with a
three column allowance for each. Thickness and width groups are punch-
ed in the first two columns following the sorting data. If a log requires two cards to show two thickness groups in 4/4" uppers, then the
commons are divided similarly. If only one width for 4/4 is needed in
the uppers, however, the common 4/4 in all shown on the same card re-
gardless of whether or not more than width group was cut. The same
holds true for the other groups. The idea is to remain within reason-
able bounds in respect to the total number of cards used and at the
same time to provide an approximation, at least, of the range in sizes
of common lumber produced from different sizes of logs.

Depreciation Study

The field forms for this subdivision of the woods and mill study
have been forwarded to Madison for punching.

Lumber Stain Project

As noted in a previous report, the field data on the 18,000 boards
inspected during the yard stain dipping experiments at Pinedale are being
held for punch carding at Madison this summer so nothing further has been
accomplished toward the organization of the final report, but a preliminary announcement was prepared for the lumber trade journals this month
by Brundage.

The tables to be published are reproduced below:

1. SAVINGS IN SELECT GRADES OF SUGAR PINE DUE TO
   DIPPING OF GREEN LUMBER BEFORE PILING IN AIR
   YARD; WINTER DRYING, FRESNO REGION.
   (Preliminary figures subject to correction.
   Not to be considered as final indices of rela-
   tive efficiency.)

SAVINGS IN DOLLARS AND CENTS PER M FT. B.M.

Chemical	Clear		C.Select	
	Slash Grain	Vertical Grain	Slash Grain	Vertical Grain
German Preparation 4/10% Solution	$ 3.90	8.05	3.68	4.54
Same,6/10% solution	4.15	10.75	5.25	3.85
K-1,3/10% solution	12.12	4.90	4.55	.70
Swedish Preparation 2.0% Sol.	6.10	9.97	7.35	9.81
Mercuric Chloride 35/100% Sol.	16.40	17.92	17.50	17.50

2. RELATIVE PERCENTAGES OF UNSTAINED PLUS VERY
   LIGHTLY STAINED (TRACE) BOARDS AFTER DRYING
   INCLUDING STOCK SHOWING 'CHEMICAL' BROWN STAIN
   ONLY.
   (Remarks above table 1 also applicable to
   these figures.

PER CENT BRIGHT PLUS TRACE BLUE PLUS BROWN (NON-FUNGUS) STAIN

Solution	All Grades Combined - 3 Shop & Better			
	Slash Grain		Vertical Grain	
	Dipped	Not Dipped	Dipped	Not Dipped
German Preparation 4/10% Solution	27	7	62	26
	(50)	(75)	(7)	(30)
Same,6/10% Sol.	32	4	78	16
	(35)	(75)	(5)	(43)
K-1, 3/10% Sol.	100	32	100	64
	(0)	(34)	(0)	(10)
Swedish Preparation 2.0% Sol.	39	2	74	10
	(8)	(78)	(2)	(47)
Mercuric Chloride 35/100% Sol.	100	4	100	3
	(0)	(92)	(0)	(69)

-- figures in parentheses show ~C -_R IR
OF COMBINED MEDIUM AND HEAVY BLUE STAIN in
each subdivision. These figures in the "UN-
DIPPED" columns are excellent measures of the
comparative original "inclination to stain" of
the various lots of test lumber. The sum of
the two figures in each block deducted from
100 will give the per cent of light stain in
each case.

Entomology

Struble is continuing his nutritional studies with the western pine
beetle and also assisting Person with reports on last season's field
studies. He completed a report on the insect losses on four check areas
for the years 1927, 1928, and part of 1929.

Person is continuing his work on reports and is also preparing plans
and materials for the coming field season. The report on biological control studies has been completed. It was found that it was possible to expose infested logs under such conditions that a very large per cent of the
D. brevicomis broods were killed without injury to any of the beneficial
predators. This method, however, is applicable only to summer control in
open stands. It is planned to test this biological control by means of an
experimental control project.

-----#-----

NORTHERN ROCKY MOUNTAIN FOREST EXPERIMENT STATION

The yield study project is now nearing completion. Several interesting developments in this study have taken place within the last month.
One is the discovery (not entirely unsuspected) that the percentage of
white pine in the stand tends to vary with site index. This tendency is
fairly well marked, the correlation index (for the relationship is curvilinear) being +.66 ±.03. For this reason pure white pine stands tend to
be higher yielding than the average mixed stand, not because of any direct effect of composition, but because such stands tend to occur on the
better sites. This relationship must still be regarded with some suspi-
cion, however, due to the relatively large influence of one local group
of plots. But even with this group eliminated, the general tendency is
still fairly well defined.

Another interesting discovery is that a high correlation exists between number of trees above certain diameter limits and the board-foot volume of the stand. The relationship between number of trees in the 13-inch class and up and board-foot volume above the same limit is +.88± .01. Trees 13 inches and up constitute the "dominant" stand, dominant and codominant trees, on the average site at about rotation age. For sampling a given stand to determine its board-foot normality and for short time predictions of the percentage of normality in the future, number of trees seems to offer an easy and rapid method of application. All it would require would be a knowledge of site and age class and a count on representative sample plots of the number of trees above a chosen diameter limit.

Thompson reports the usual heavy rush of work at this time of year at the Priest River Branch. The model plantation was replanted to fill in all blanks and some planting of arboretum stock was done also. The station fire break was plowed and some experimental sowings of fire resistant plants are now under way. The bi-weekly phenological observations of three plots were commenced for the 1930 season. The usual repair and maintenance work on the eight station buildings and other structures, which consumes a considerable portion of the local officer's time, has been proceeding satisfactorily. Thompson has also started the formation of a Branch Station photograph collection.

-----#-----

PACIFIC NORTHWEST FOREST EXPERIMENT STATION

Letter-size Outline Map

The four tracings to be used in the printing of a letter-size outline map of the Station's territory were completed and sent to the printer. They include the names and boundaries of national forests, counties, and states, as well as the important cities and drainages. The map will be printed in four colors, black, green, blue, and red. It was so designed as to meet the need of several agencies who expect to use it for quite a variety of purposes.

Douglas Fir Reproduction Studies

During the early part of April Isaac started the nursery germination tests of seeds stored in the duff. The seed being tested this year has been in the duff for the past two seasons. A similar test conducted from 1925 to 1929 showed no germination after the first year. The Douglas fir spacing test plantation, now in its fifth year, was photographed and the dead trees replaced. A loss of 3 per cent occurred since April 1929. Many 4-year-old trees were found dead, drouth being the cause. In a thrifty part of the 4x4 spacing the side branches nearly touch. Here the canopy will be closed in a few years and the shrub and herbaceous growth crowded out. The tallest trees on the area are seven feet in height and last year one tree bore a well-developed cone containing a considerable number of sound seed.

Examinations were made of plots established to test germination of seed in place under virgin timber and in the open. Also germination tests of noble fir seed held in cold storage were started. The test of noble fir seed held in cold storage is now in its fourth year. The germination has dropped from 21 per cent the first year to 15 per cent the third year, while part of the same lot of seed stored at room temperature showed no germination after the first year.

Methods of Cutting

Kólbe spent the greater part of his time in the preparation of progress reports on the several methods of cutting plots. Volume computations are now being made for plots that had been held up for a number of years for lack of suitable volume tables.

Mensuration

The work on cubic volume for western yellow pine started about two months ago is now completed. Four tables, one for each of the lower four out of five site classes of the regional western yellow pine volume tables, were prepared. In addition the board foot tables in merchantable heights were converted to tables expressed in total height. A study of the length of top above the 8-inch diameter gave the basis for conversion. A separate cubic foot table was constructed for immature pine in Oregon. All of the new tables, together with the tables worked by the Washington Office, form a set which ought to have many uses in the entire western yellow pine region.

Some of the winter's work has culminated in preparation of five reports, one of them dealing with volume tables mentioned above, one on a set of thinning plots in sapling Douglas fir which has been under observation for ten years, and three on permanent sample plots in even-aged Douglas fir second growth on several of the D-6 forests. The western yellow pine growth and yield project is not represented in the list of reports, although it occupied a majority of the computational time throughout the winter.

Two short trips were made during April, one for the purpose of remeasuring three yield plots on the Cascade Forest, established twenty years ago, and another to the Mt. Hood Forest to establish new plots. Three plots representing different grades of stocking were laid out in a 45-year-old stand.

Wind River

On April 2 Simson again took up his residence at the Wind River Branch Station. Since then he has been largely engaged in getting the Station into operation and doing the annual spring work. With the aid of one of the District tractors a 20-foot fireline was built along the south side of the arboretum.

For several years there has been an increasing amount of damage by rodents in the arboretum. Last fall Mr. Leo Couch of the Bureau of Biological Survey came to the rescue and staged an intensive campaign of trapping and poisoning. Altogether about 100 pounds of poisoned grain was put out. This month Mr. Couch returned to check up on the results of the work. Very few signs of either gophers or mice were found.

Forest Survey

The Forest Survey staff was increased April 1 by the addition of Junior Forester Edward D. Buell by transfer from District 5.

Granger, Munger, Andrews, and Mathews, after conference with the District Office, completed the final instructions for the preparation of the 1930 timber inventory of the national forests for the Douglas fir region, and the instructions were mimeographed and distributed to the various forests.

Andrews devoted considerable time to the detailed working plan for the private lands and field methods. Several short field trips were made by Andrews, Briegleb, and Hoffman to test out the procedure.

Cowlin, Moravets, and Buell spent two weeks gathering preliminary data at the county seats in southern and central Washington getting complete information on county cruises, maps showing ownership, areas covered by the county cruise and cut over. On this trip the district fire wardens in this region were seen and arrangements made for them to make general type maps of their respective territories. J. D. Lacey & Company and Porteous & Company, forest engineers and timber cruisers, were seen and maps made of the areas cruised by Lacey & Company in western Oregon and western Washington.

-----#-----

Fire

Pessin and Wyman burned the spring plot in the series of longleaf fire plots at McNeill.

The Raiford fire plots, on which a test is being made of the turpentine yield of burned and unburned plots, were fenced to keep hogs from rubbing against the trees and knocking off the cups.

Management

Pessin reports interesting contrasts from the Chapman Forest (longleaf pine) at Urania, part of which was burned prior to the 1928 seed fall, and part left unburned. After the 1928 seed fall fewer seedlings started on the unburned side than on the burned, but after a year in the field the seedlings on the unburned side show a much higher survival. In 1929 a second heavy seed crop, germinating early in October, resulted in a heavy stand of seedlings on both sides, but some adverse factor, probably last winter's extreme cold, has now reduced the stand from the 1929 crop to about 3,000 seedlings per acre on both the burned and unburned sides. Pessin is hand weeding small plots on the unburned side to learn the effect upon longleaf seedlings of reducing competing vegetation without introducing the harmful effects of fire.

Chapman and May helped the Laboratory crew finish the loblolly logging and milling study at Urania, tallied the remaining stand, and recorded the pulpwood cut from tops.

Chapman also spent some time on the Ouachita Forest looking for possible method-of-cutting and increased-growth areas, and discussing marking and silvicultural practice with the Forest personnel. From the Ouachita he continued to the Crossett Lumber Company's holdings in Arkansas, still looking for method-of-cutting areas.

On the Ouachita Chapman checked the silvicultural improvement plots, finding that the arsenic poisons applied to competing hardwoods had been pretty effective except on black gum, and that the other poisons had been less effective.

At Camp Pinchot Gemmer and Bennett located specific areas for a method-of-cutting study in longleaf pine, and practically completed intensive cruises of the various plots. They also set up additional instruments, including dendrometers, for the study of environment on the Laboratory and other plots.

Naval Stores

The first gum dip of the season was made at Starke. Gum samples
from this first dip were sent to the Bureau of Chemistry and Soils for a
determination of the percentages of turpentine, rosin, water, and trash.
Samples from the same groups were sent last year and the results showed
that longleaf gum had a higher percentage of turpentine than slash.
This was contrary to the popular belief that slash gum contained more
turpentine, a belief that was doubtless based on the more liquid character of the slash pine gum. Analyses of the gum samples this year will
show for some groups what the effect of not raising the cups will have
on the percentage of turpentine and for other groups they will show what
variations in percentage of turpentine and rosin occur for the different
seasons.

Considerable progress was made in five-year remeasurements of
trees, face-healing and rate of growth measurements.

Forestation

Wakeley, with Meginnis' help, completed the regular annual reexamination of 21 acres of experimental plantations at Bogalusa. He later
helped Craig and Miss Regan transcribe the last of the reexamination notes,
which were then transmitted to Washington for punching.

At Bogalusa weekly phenological examinations of some 200 planted
longleaf seedlings showed conclusively that the less vigorous seedlings,
such as develop from the poorer grades of nursery stock, start growth
earlier in the spring than do the more vigorous. In extreme cases, brown_
spot infections on the 1930 foliage of weak seedlings had progressed to
the fruiting stage of the fungus before the buds of vigorous seedlings
had opened enough to expose any 1930 foliage whatever.

Gemmer reports complete loss of longleaf pine planted last winter
at East Bay Ranger Station on the Choctawhatchee, probably as a result
of drying when heeled in.

In the Camp Pinchot nursery one slash pine seed bed was completely destroyed by doves one morning between dawn and six o'clock, and had
to be resown.

Protection, Others

An infestation of Ips in the logging slash from the Kingsley thinning plots at Starke made it advisable to pile and burn the tops and limbs.
The cord-wood that had been cut and piled was removed from the plots.

Economics

Ziegler, Bond, and Spillers continued work on the reports, original or revised, on Appling County, Georgia; Lee County, Alabama; and Alcorn County, Mississippi.

Bond left on April 28 for North Carolina to cooperate with the Taxation Inquiry in the study of Beaufort County.

Erosion

The first week in April was spent in the office at New Orleans working up the erosion reports for Adams and Jefferson Counties.

At the end of the Southern Forestry Congress Lentz and Demmon took Associate Forester E. A. Sherman over some of the worst eroded country in northern Mississippi.

Following the Forestry Congress Lentz, Sinclair, and Meginnis made a three day trip into western Tennessee with State Forester Maddox to study gully control work. Through the construction of brush dams followed by plowing off some of the good top soil in which locust could be planted, the majority of the gullies worked on were controlled. The most difficult factor Mr. Maddox had to contend with was lack of cooperation on the part of the landowner.

Several days were spent getting erosion data in Carroll County which ranks next to Marshall and Lafayette County in the seriousness of the erosion taking place.

Pathology

Siggers planted on the Alabama National Forest approximately 3200 Asiatic chestnut seedlings shipped there from Washington as part of a study of possible blight-resistant species. He also sprayed the Bogalusa brown spot plots, and noted differences in development of new foliage between the sprayed and the unsprayed plots. Among the smaller longleaf seedlings, growth started earlier on the check plots, on which there had been no control of brown spot by spraying.

At Clarks, La., Lindgren and Scheffer started another small scale dipping test in the series of tests in connection with blue stain prevention in southern pine and sap gum lumber. Notes were taken on the results of similar tests run at Laurel, Mississippi, and Chapman, Alabama. Some preliminary log spray and end coating tests aimed at the prevention of stain in gum logs were begun at Opelousas, Louisiana.

SOUTHWESTERN FOREST EXPERIMENT STATION

An event of unusual scientific interest was the annual meeting of the Southwestern Division of the American Association for the Advancement of Science, in Tucson April 21 - 25. One of the best programs was that of the Southwestern Section of the Society of American Foresters. Lowdermilk of the California Forest Experiment Station gave two papers on the watershed problem. Mortality in western yellow pine stands was the subject of a paper by Krauch. Pearson talked on forests and climate in a symposium on Solar-Terrestrial Relations in the Section of Physical Sciences.

Immediately following the meetings of the Association, President Shantz held a Conference on Wild Life, Forest, and Range Problems. Invitations to attend this conference had been issued to educational and scientific institutions, government and State agencies, civic organizations, and industrial associations. Between 40 and 50 representatives attended the meeting. Dr. Shantz outlined briefly the conservation problems confronting the Southwest, pointing out the need for intelligent husbanding of natural resources if this region is to avert the fate of former desert civilizations. Expressions from various representatives indicated a sympathetic attitude, though not always an adequate understanding of the situation. As a preliminary step in studying the problems at hand, Dr. Shantz advocated a comprehensive research project involving cooperation between State, government, and other research agencies. The purpose of the investigations would be to make a thorough study of climate and soil, and the reactions of vegetation to the factors of their environment. In brief, it would be a repetition on a grand scale of the "Forest Type" projects which have been carried on by the Forest Service in Districts 1, 2 and 3. The meeting was divided into three groups, representing wild life, forestry, and grazing interests. These groups endorsed Dr. Shantz's program individually and jointly. A committee headed by Dr. Shantz, and containing one member from each of the three groups, was appointed for the purpose of continuing the activity instituted by the conference. The members of this committee are: wild life, Walter P. Taylor of the Biological Survey; forestry, G. A. Pearson of the Southwestern Forest Experiment Station; range, W. G. McGinnies of the University of Arizona. It was later decided that water resources should be represented on this committee, but the representative was not named.

It is understood that the primary purpose of the committee is to maintain interest in the program and to promote cooperation between different research agencies. It will have no administrative functions.

The first step in the program is the establishement and operation of a series of physical-biological stations in the principal life zones extending from the desert to the upper limit of tree growth. These stations will be organized and financed on a cooperative basis. The individual stations may be operated entirely by one organization or institution, or by two or more in cooperation. All should be standardized as to basic equipment and measurement of factors. This standardization obviously calls for very careful planning. Presumably this will be one of the functions of the above committee. The University of Arizona contemplates establishing one complete station in the near future, and others as funds become available. The Desert Laboratory and the Boyce-Thompson Southwestern Arboretum will probably maintain sub-stations supplementing a main desert station. It should be the aim of the Southwestern Forest Experiment Station, as soon as funds become available, to establish a complete station in the western yellow pine type, and sub-stations in the Douglas fir and Engelmann spruce types.

It should be made clear that the purpose of these stations is to obtain fundamental data of broad application, rather than to work out specific problems. The records will supply the basic data needed in a great many investigations, such as the requirements of trees and forage plants, growth, reproduction and competition, natural distribution of plants and animals, water supply and erosion; but each of these investigations will require additional records of a specialized nature though usually of relatively short duration.

Since the primary purpose of the stations is to measure the physical factors in typical plant habitats, the preservation of natural vegetation around each station is assumed. It has been suggested that the stations be located within Research reserves or natural areas now being set aside by the Forest Service. This is desirable but not always practical because the physical-biological stations must be readily accessible. For example, the most practical location of the Douglas fir and Engelmann spruce stations is at a convenient distance from the San Francisco Mts. Boulevard. Small bodies of virgin forest occur near the road, but really typical bodies of forest such as would be selected to represent natural conditions occur only on the other side of the mountain, about two miles from the nearest point accessible by automobile. Moreover, it is conceivable that some investigations involving disturbance of natural vegetation may need to be located near the stations in order to take advantage of climatic records of immediate applicability. This problem deserves thoughtful consideration, along with that of life zones to be represented, the character of records and types of equipment.

-----#-----

April Activities

Prior to the start of active field work at Fremont, Roeser prepared a working plan for the future conduct of the seed production experiment with Douglas fir. The results obtained in this study in 1925 and 1926 were tabulated and plàtted in order to correlate, if possible, flower emergence and production with climatic conditions, principally minimum temperature, which might influence the development of the very young flowers. The data, to date, apparently substantiate the theory that climatic conditions play an important part in determining the ratio of cone to flower production, but two conditions seem to operate as limiting factors, namely frost, and foggy weather, which either freeze the blossoms or limit pollen dissemination.

At Fremont, the first work consisted of establishing a soil well at each of the fourteen field meteorological stations at which observations are regularly made in the type study. Additional instruments were also placed at each station, in order to enlarge the scope of observations beginning May 1.

Preliminary effort in planting activities involved the setting out of 300, 2-2, western yellow pine trees representing two parent trees in the heredity study. A somewhat smaller number of Douglas firs of the same age, and in the same project, are also available, but planting of these has been postponed until early May.

Rangers Varney and Leadbeater completed the tabulation of field data and the preparation of stand tables for the bulk of the District management study plots, about the middle of the month. The former then moved to the Fremont Station where he assisted in getting the spring work started, and in the spring cutting operations on the experimental forest. An attempt will be made to complete the cutting, as soon as possible, on Block A, one of the four working units into which the Forest has been divided.

Leadbeater was assigned the task of compiling the climatological data procured during the 1929 field season at Fremont.

No reports were received from the Nebraska Forest, but it is assumed that spring operations in connection with experimental stock at the Halsey Nursery followed in line with the instructions contained in the recently prepared supplemental working plan.

-----#-----

MANUSCRIPTS

LAKE STATES

"Second-Growth White Pine in Wisconsin - Its Growth Yield and Commercial Possibilities." S. R. Govorkiantz and Raphael Zon. (To Wis. Agr. Expt. Sta., for Res. Bul.)

CALIFORNIA

In Instrument to Measure Water Losses by Evaporation and Transpiration from Drained Slopes. W. C. Lowdermilk.

Certain Problems in the Management of Watersheds for Maximum Beneficial Water Production. W. C. Lowdermilk.

Forestry in Denuded China, W. C. Lowdermilk (For Annals of Amer. Acad, of Political and Social Science).

Orientation of the Water Use Problem from the Forester's Point of View. C. L. Hill (For A. S. C. E. Meeting on Consumptive Use of Water, Los Angeles, March 27, 1930).

APPALACHIAN

The Sout.ern Appalachian Spruce Forest as Affected by Logging and Fire. C. F. Korstian (For Tech. Bul.)

Effects of 1925 Summer Drought on Southern Appalachian Hardwoods. By C. R. Hursh and F. W. Haasis (For Ecology)

Further Experiments with Blue-stain Fungi in Southern Pines. R. M. Nelson (Thesis for Ph.D. degree)

ALLEGHENY

Tags and Painted Numbers on Trees in Permanent Sample Plots. By H. F Morey, (For Jour. of Forestry)

PACIFIC NORTHWEST

The Effect of Relative Humidity on Short-Period Fluctuations in Fuel Moisture Content. By A. G. Simson.

Forest Planting Progress in Washington and Oregon. By Leo A. Isaac.
(For West Coast Lumberman)

Relative Humidity and Fuel Moisture, by A. G. Simson. (For Four L
Lumber News).

Manuscript Reports by W. H. Meyer:

    "Volume Tables for Western Yellow Pine."

    "First Report on Rainier Permanent Sample Plots in Second-
    growth Douglas fir."

    "Report on the 1929 Measurements of the Permanent Sample
    Plots 2, 4, 5, and 9, Columbia National Forest."

    "First Report on Permanent Sample Plots 10, 11, and 12,
    Columbia National Forest."

    "Report on the Third Measurement of the Piedmont Thinning
    Plots, Wind River Branch Station."

IN PRINT

Bates, C. G.   "Why Nursery men Prefer Souther Seeds" (Jour. For.
        Feb. 1930.

        Review of: "Races of Douglas Fir and Sitka Spruce"
                by A. Oppermann. (Jour. For. Feb. 1930)

        Review of: "The Varieties and Geographical Forms of
                Pinus pinaster Soland, in Europe and
                South Africa," by C. E. Duff. (Jour.
                For. Feb. 1930)

Brundage, M. R. "Dipping Treatments Show Substantial Saving in Yard
        Stain Losses." (Amer. Lumberman, April 5, 1930).

Forbes, R. D.   "What Uncle Sam Does to Solve the Forest Problem."
        (Engineers and Engineering, April,1930, Phila.,Pa.)

Gisborne, H. T. "How Dangerous are Dry Lightning Storms?" (Northwest
        Science, March, 1930)

Hursh, C. R.   "Forestation Averts Erosion on Abandoned Mountain
        Farm Land. (Yearbook, 1930)

Lindgren, R. M. "The Determination of Logs in Storage and Its Prevention." (Southern Lumberman, March 15, 1930).

"   "   "Industrial Research and the Forestry School." (The
Gopher Peavy, 1930)

Meyer, W. H.   Review of: "The Reaction of Swamps to Drainage in
Northern Minnesota," by J. L. Averell
and P. C. McGrew (Jour. For. Feb. 1930).

"   "   Review of: "Drainage of Swamps and Forests Growth,"
by R. Zon and J. L. Averell (Jour. For.
Feb. 1930)

Munger, T. T. "Inventorying Oregon's Forest Wealth" (Oregon Bank-
ing Bulletin).

Rudolf, Paul   "Some Phases of Forest Management in the Southern
Turpentine Region." (The Gopher Peavy, 1930).

Tillotson, C. R. Review of: "Field Book of Destructive Forest Insects,"
by H. B. Peirson.

-----#-----

Timber Survey

The five-year revision of the data for this project was started during the winter of 1928 and 1929. The work was done largely by contributed time and consisted of a revision of the status and type maps for northern Idaho counties. Ranger Robb of the Missoula Forest spent 37 effective days on this work during the past winter. All of his time was devoted to further revision of the figures for North Idaho. With a limited amount of contributed time available and no funds it seems best at this time to concentrate our work in North Idaho for several reasons. First, the original data for Idaho were quite inaccurate. There is also a greater need at this time for more dependable information in the white pine type than in other parts of the region. Furthermore, the rate of change in forest cover of North Idaho, due to logging and fires, is much faster than in Montana.

Data on timber estimates and Forest area classifications of the National Forests in the District were also brought up to date during the winter by the Office of Forest Management.

Census

Returns have been received from at least 75 per cent of the establishments in Idaho and Montana, but there are still about 175 names on the directory lists which it will be necessary to clear up through personal interviews and additional requests by mail. It is expected to secure reports from most of these delinquents during the next three or four weeks. The final clean-up work will be started about May 15.

Production reports received from the large mills cutting 5,000 M or more in 1929 indicate an increase of approximately 7 per cent in the combined cut of the two States as compared with the preceding year.

The following comparison is based on the output of identical mills which contributed 85.7 per cent of the total cut reported in 1928:

State	No. of Mills	Lumber Cut (M Feet Board Measure)	
		1929	1930
Montana	10	331,931	322,514
Idaho	23	925,094	848,814
Totals	33	1,257,025	1,171,328

The 33 mills included in this tabulation were operated by 28 different companies of which only 11 show any reduction in output as compared with 1928. Seventeen of these establishments produced more lumber than in 1928.

A large number of schedules edited during the month of April will be forwarded to Washington within a few days.

Anaconda Wood Preservative Paste.

The wood preservative that was originally introduced under the name of "Cold Treater Dust" is now being marketed by the Anaconda Copper Mining Company in three forms, namely, dust, granules and paste. According to a statement from Mr. Caro of this company the paste has been developed particularly for use on new as well as old set poles in dry soils and on old set poles in both dry and wet soils so that a movement of the arsenic into the wood will begin as soon as the paste is applied to the pole. The paste is said to contain from 60 to 62 per cent arsenic trioxide (As_2O_3), about 26 per cent water and 1/2 per cent Irish moss.

A description of this new form of the preservative and specifications for applying it are contained in the company's Bulletin No. 6 "Anaconda Wood Preservative and Weed Killer" of January, 1930. A number of copies of this bulletin have been obtained from Dr. H. C. Gardiner of the Anaconda Copper Mining Company with the following statement in a letter dated April 23:

"You will note that this bulletin deals exclusively with the Anaconda Wood Preservative Paste, which is the form we now recommend altogether for this western territory where rains are not frequent and ground moisture cannot be depended on to be sufficient to start an immediate absorption of Preservative up and into the pole or post when dry forms of the material are used. On the other hand, the toxic moisture content of the Paste gives this primary treatment that prevents rot getting started in the wood. Furthermore, by being able to plaster it on the treated surface gives a more complete and efficient treatment. This is particularly true of the treatment of old poles or posts where the Paste can be smeared into holes and checks after rot has been completely cleaned and scraped off and for the treatment of old poles or posts in place we recommend the Paste exclusively."

The present prices per pound for Anaconda Wood Preservative and Anaconda Week Killer f.o.b. stocks Anaconda, Montana, are as follows:

Lots	Wood Preservative		Weed Killer	
	Granules	Paste	(Cans)	(Drums)
Less than 500 lbs.	7¢	6¢	7¢	5¢
500 to 2,000 lbs.	6.5	5.5	6.5	4.5
2,000 lbs. up	6	5	6	4

Minimum order Wood Preservative two cases Granules, 120 lbs. or
two buckets Paste, 100 pounds.

Minimum order Weed Killer, three cases (cans), 90 lbs., or two
drums, 150 pounds.

The first Forest Service test with the paste form of Anaconda
Wood Preservative in this District was installed on the Missoula Forest
during the past month. It includes about 60 new telephone poles treated
by District Ranger A. C. Austin at the time of setting.

Lumber Prices

Av. Mill-Run Prices	Annual, 1928	Annual, 1929	January, 1930	February, 1930	March, 1930
Idaho White Pine	$31.09	$34.33	$36.21	$35.21	$35.12
Western Yellow Pine	24.51	26.17	24.15	24.24	25.34
Larch-Fir	18.55	20.29	19.48	18.64	17.37
White Fir	18.26	20.94	19.24	17.52	21.51
Spruce	23.20	24.23	23.28	24.94	22.99

Miscellaneous Reports

The annual Manufacturing Costs and the first quarter Lumber Prices
were compiled by Mrs. Bullard during April.

-----#-----

OFFICE OF PRODUCTS, D-6

General

Mr. Gibbons left Portland on April 24 to attend the annual allot-
ment conference at the Madison Laboratory. He expects to return to this
office about May 15.

Having completed their studies in kiln drying Douglas fir, at
least for this season, at Vernonia, Oregon; Messrs. Loughborough and
Rietz stopped in at the office on their return to the Laboratory at Madison, Wisconsin.

Survey of Sawmill Waste in the Douglas Fir Region

Mr. Hodgson spent most of the month on this project in the office. With the assistance of a temporary clerk he was able to work the results of one shift at one of the hemlock sawmills studied last February through to completion. This was done to perfect the office technique and to secure a check on the general approach adopted by the working plan for the intensive study of sawmill waste. As it worked out the volume of lumber, waste wood in its various forms, sawdust and bark as computed from measurements checked remarkably well when compared with the volume of wood and bark contained in the logs which were sawed during the period of study.

The summary showing results of this study shift was divided into the following headings under which are shown pertinent figures and tables: "Logs Sawed and Lumber Produced", "Segregation of Sound Wood Contained in the Logs into Lumber, Waste Wood and Sawdust", "Segregation of Bark Contained in the Logs into Waste and Sawdust", "Present Utilization (commercial lumber, domestic power, wood for pulp chips, wood and bark for hogged fuel and wood sent to refuse burner) of Material Contained in Logs" and "Distribution of Waste (solid wood and sawdust) to the Various Saws".

This check-up on the methods adopted both in the field and office having proved them to be satisfactory, the office work now resolves itself to the routine work of computing and tabulating the results for the other seven shifts which were studied in the four hemlock sawmills selected for intensive study and worked in last February.

A considerable part of Hodgson's time was also spent in editing the questionnaire returns "Census of So-Called Sawmill Waste, 1929" which have been filled out and sent in by most of the sawmills of the Douglas fir region. The data from these returns will provide some very valuable information regarding the present utilization of sawmill waste and its value, in the form of by-products made from it, in dollars and cents. These data, representing statistics which have never been collected before and regarding which very little is known, will be used in Hodgson's final report relating to "Sawmill Waste and Its Present Utilization in the Douglas Fir Region".

Western Yellow Pine Utilization Studies

Mr. Spelman spent the entire month on office work, most of which was devoted to work relating to the Mt. Emily and Shevlin-Hixon mill-scale studies. One of the outstanding differences between the results of the Mt. Emily mill-scale study and the Shevlin-Hixon study is the over-run. Comparing only the sound logs in the two studies, the average over-run for the Mt. Emily logs was 21.4 per cent as against 15.1 per cent for the Shevlin-Hixon logs. Throughout the entire range of diameter classes the Mt. Emily logs had a consistently higher over-run.

Preliminary analysis of the over-run in the Mt. Emily mill-scale study indicates that taper is an important factor only in the lower diameter classes. The results seem to indicate that for 16-ft. logs, the increase in over-run per 2" increase in taper ranged from 16 per cent in 8" logs to about 3 per cent in 18" logs. In the larger diameters (above 18"), the effect of taper was rather slight. In other words, if an 8" log with two inches taper has an over-run of 40 per cent, an 8" log with 4 inches taper would have about 56 per cent over-run. Likewise an 8" log with 6 inches taper would have an over-run of about 72 per cent.

The work in connection with the Shevlin-Hixon study was done for the purpose of determining marginal values in different parts of trees of different sizes. The problem consists of comparing the lumber value of logs in different positions in the tree with the cost of logging and milling them. The plan is to make a second report on this study covering this phase of utilization, with the intention of indicating the relative value of the top log material.

Census of Lumber, Lath, Shingles, Logs, Cooperage and Veneer

Third requests were sent to 512 companies in Oregon and Washington who are on the regular list which is canvassed each year. In addition, third requests were sent to 812 so-called "new" companies, making a total of 1324.

A great deal of correspondence has been necessary in an endeavor to secure complete returns, which results in slowing up the work considerably.

A total of 285 companies on our regular list still remain to be heard from.

Cooperation

Mr. Johnson spent the entire month in cooperation with the Bureau of Census on the 1929 log, lumber, and other timber products census. A total of 550 schedules were edited. Of these 276 Washington and 167 Oregon schedules were good. Some time was spent in Portland and vicinity picking up delinquent companies.

Publications

On April 5 Mr. Hodgson presented a paper, entitled "Logging Waste - A Challenge to the Pulp Industry of the Douglas Fir Region" at the Spring meeting of the Pacific Coast Section of the American Pulp and Paper Industry held at Longview, Washington. The paper reviewed the principal

findings of the survey "Logging Waste in the Douglas Fir Region" and
- pointed out reasons why it would be to the ultimate advantage of the
local pulp industry to make use of the tremendous quantities of poten-
tial pulpwood which is now being wasted by logging operations.

Notification was received from the editor of "The Paper Industry"
of Chicago, that Hodgson's paper together with five illustrations furnished by this office is to be published in full in the April issue of
that Journal.

-----#-----

FOREST TAXATION INQUIRY

The annual Program Conference was held on April 4 and 5, being attended by Messrs. Clapp, Marsh, and Ziegler. In addition to discussing the various individual projects now under way and contemplated in the near future, some consideration was given to plans for a comprehensive report in which the conclusions of the Inquiry will appear. It was forecast that this report will be published in a series of bulletins. Plans for continuation of work on forest taxation after the issuing of the comprehensive report were discussed in a general way.

Arrangements begun at the Program Conference and since made effective have resulted in a cooperative attack on the forestry situation in Beaufort County, North Carolina, by Dr. Ziegler's staff in the Southern Forest Experiment Station studying the financial aspects of forestry and by the Inquiry. Mr. Bond, representing the "financial aspects" study, has joined Messrs. Wager and Thomson in the field. This joint attack is expected to be mutually advantageous.

A study of the public finances of forest communities as contrasted with agricultural communities in the same state has been commenced by Dr. Allin in a number of eastern states where the financial information is readily available. The results of the study will serve to supplement the more detailed financial studies which the Inquiry has made in certain of the states which have been selected for special investigation.

Machine compilation of the data that are coming in from the North Carolina field party has begun, an extra punch card operator having been employed to expedite the punching of the Hollerith cards.

In connection with the North Carolina project, the cooperation of the Southern Railway was obtained so that the Inquiry could get the benefit of sales data in Chatham County which are being collected by the local valuation experts in the employ of the Railway.

-----#-----

WASHINGTON

Secretary Approves Establishment of Southwestern Forest and Range Experiment Station

The Secretary of Agriculture has approved the establishment of the Southwestern Forest and Range Experiment Station with headquarters at the University of Arizona, Tucson, Arizona. This will make possible the centralization of the various units now in the Southwest, doubtless including the range research on the National Forests in District 3, Jornada and Santa Rita Range Reserves, and the silvicultural research located at Flagstaff.

Publications

Campbell's "Plant Succession and Grazing Capacity on Clay Soils in Southern New Mexico", designed for publication in the Journal of Agricultural Research, was received and has been sent to the various members of the Board of Review for their consideration. This manuscript is of particular value in that it brings out the successional trends on the moving sand areas which tend to scour away the clay soils and then gradually sweep over them in slowly moving dunes.

Forsling resubmitted the revised manuscript "Artificial Reseeding of Western Mt. Ranges" and it was turned over to Dayton, the co-author, for his final consideration and approval. This manuscript aims to present in concise, practical form the present status of our artificial reseeding investigations and the opportunities which they indicate there are for seeding the better type of range land.

Erosion Reconnaissance Data Machine Tabulated

Director Forsling of the Great Basin Station sent in a preliminary test run of the material covering the erosion reconnaissance on the Boise River watershed. Machine tabulations indicated that there are certain general relationships between density of vegetation, degree of slope, intensity of rodent infestation and degree of seriousness of erosion. This preliminary run indicated certain general adjustments that should be made in the future coding and analysis of the data.

Visitors

Dan Campbell of Campbell and Francis Sheep Company, Flagstaff, Arizona, dropped in the office to consider the studies under way in Arizona. He was in Washington in connection with the consideration of certain matters affecting the Company.

Mr. John T. Caine, III, of the International Livestock Exposition, Chicago, Illinois, came in the office to discuss Forest Service participation in the Department's exhibit for next fall's exposition and also the status of range investigations in the West.

Film Strip Range Management Lecture to be Developed

Mr. C. H. Hanson of the Section of Visual Instruction and Editorial Work of the Office of Cooperative Extension, called at the office for a conference in regard to the revision of the range management lantern-slide lecture prepared by Chapline several years ago. Mr. Hanson suggested that the lecture be revised on the basis of film strip, both because of the saving in storage space, the convenience of shipment, and operation. This film strip would be made up from photographs selected specifically to represent the various management practices. Since the film strip can not be colored it is essential that the photographs used for making it be unusually good. The field is accordingly being called upon to secure, if possible, during this summer photographs of specific features of management that are particularly needed.

RANGE FORAGE INVESTIGATIONS

Accomplishments during April included marking in cooperation with the Civil Service Commission of the three botanical phases of the Junior Range Examiner examination, efficiency ratings, necessary odds-and-ends in connection with publications and, particularly, getting about two-thirds completed and entered on cards the index to the browse bulletin, as revised. This index has now been typed through letter D and this part takes 44 typewritten pages, from which some idea of the size of the job can be obtained.

Call from Dr. Smith

On April 21st we were favored with a visit from Dr. C. Piper Smith, the well-known authority on lupines, who is on his way to England for a visit. Prof. Smith states that he has decided to enlarge his monograph of lupines from an American to a world-wide basis, and to try to issue it in 1935, the centenary of Agardh's lupine treatise, the last revision of the genus.

-41-

Plant Identification

Twenty-two collections, representing 937 specimens, were sent to the Bureau of Plant Industry in April for formal determination. 312 specimens were filed in the herbarium and 30 mounted.

-----#-----

JORNADA RANGE RESERVE

Conditions Looking up

While precipitation on the whole is still light and very spotted, a few heavy rains over the eastern part of the reserve have filled some of the surface tanks to overflowing. Forage growth is good for this time of year, the cattle are in good condition, and an excellent calf crop is in view.

Forage Analysis

Material of Bouteloua eriopoda and B. curtipendula was furnished to Prof. A. W. Sampson of the University of California for initial forage analysis. Further samples of the same species will be collected at different intervals during the season, in an effort to secure data on seasonal variability of nutrients in some of the chief grass species on the Jornada.

Visitors

Mr. H. H. Bennett, of the Bureau of Chemistry and Soils, and Prof. J. L. Lantow of the State Agricultural College stopped at the reserve late in the month. Mr. Bennett is particularly interested in soil erosion and is making a preliminary examination of erosion conditions in parts of the West.

Mr. and Mrs. R. R. Hill from Washington were visitors on Easter Sunday.

-----#-----

SANTA RITA RANGE RESERVE

Meetings

During the week of April 21 - 25, the Southwestern Division of the American Association for the Advancement of Science held its annual meeting at the University of Arizona in Tucson with some 150 members in attendance. The program was arranged by Prof. Wm. G. McGinnies and presented a great variety of lectures, informal symposiums, field trips, and social activities that served to keep the interest of everyone at the highest possible pitch until the very end. The final day was given over to field trips entirely and 40 people made the trip to the Santa Rita Range Reserve where the work of the station was explained. Dr. Vorhies and Dr. Taylor also discussed the rodent problems and talks were given by Dr. Ball and Prof. McGinnies.

On Saturday following the Science meeting there was held a conference, called by Dr. Shantz, for the purpose of considering wild life, forest and range problems and of developing a comprehensive program for research in the Southwest. Over 60 delegates attended the conference from various institutions and organizations throughout the region and some very interesting statements of problems were given. The delegates were divided into sections in accordance with their interests, about 25 each in wild life and range sections with something like a dozen representing forest problems. Committees were appointed in each section to develop a program and to keep all members in touch with developments.

An outstanding feature of the meeting was the keen interest shown in Dr. Shantz's proposed climatic-factor stations.

All in all the conference was a decided success and represents the first real attempt to bring together all the interests for a comprehensive discussion of the problems facing research in the region.

Miscellaneous Notes

Range continues in very good condition with an appreciable growth of perennial grasses and spring annuals occurring over most of the reserve. Very little rain has fallen during the month and apparently our spring dry season is on though it should not prove at all serious this year. Stock are in normal condition now and should be above average to enter the summer season.

-----#-----

Lightning Source UK Ltd.
Milton Keynes UK
UKHW012330061118
331891UK00010B/983/P